MW00929214

To Whom Much is Given

Navigating the Ten Life Dilemmas Affluent Christians Face

A Stewardship Guide to Wise Decision Making

I TIMOTHY 6:17-19

E. G. "Jay" Link

XULON PRESS

Copyright © 2009 by E. G. "Jay" Link

To Whom Much is Given
by E. G. "Jay" Link

Printed in the United States of America

ISBN 978-1-61579-017-3

All rights reserved solely by the author. The author guarantees all contents are original and do not infringe upon the legal rights of any other person or work. Contents and/or cover may not be reproduced in whole or in part in any form without the express written consent of the author. The views expressed in this book are not necessarily those of the publisher.

Manuscript edited by Bethany Link, Rick Killian.

Unless otherwise indicated, scripture quotations are taken from the *New American Standard Bible®,* Copyright © 1960, 1962, 1963, 1968, 1971, 1972, 1973, 1975, 1977, 1995 by The Lockman Foundation. Used by permission. (www.Lockman.org)

Scripture quotations marked NIV are taken from the *Holy Bible, New International Version®.* NIV®. Copyright © 1973, 1978, 1984, by International Bible Society. Used by permission of Zondervan. All rights reserved.

Scripture quotations marked NLT are taken from *The Holy Bible, New Living Translation.* Copyright © 1996. Used by permission of Tyndale House Publishers, Inc., Wheaton, Illinois 60189. All rights reserved.

www.xulonpress.com

Printed in the United States of America

16 15 14 13 12 11 10 09   1 2 3 4 5 6 7 8 9 10

Jay's decades of experience in working with wealthy families show through in this book as he "cuts to the chase" in identifying the major challenges and dilemmas that are common roadblocks for affluent Christian families. Jay has personally guided our family successfully through some of these very challenges and once we resolved them, it has made all the difference in our ability to plan for our family and for the Kingdom. If you have achieved a good level of financial success in life, this little book is concentrated wisdom that you simply cannot afford to be without!

John Bandimere, Owner and President,
Bandimere Speedway, Inc.

If you are struggling to know how to most wisely steward the wealth that God has entrusted to you, this book will help you clear away the "fog" of uncertainty and indecision. Jay has provided an invaluable road map to point the way on what to do with and about your wealth. It was practical, informative and helpful for me.

Hugh Maclellan, Jr., President,
Maclellan Foundation, Inc.

Jay has composed one of those rare books that combines simplicity, wisdom, and practicality. His insights and unique experience will open up the minds, and plenty of options, for the reader with substantial finances and a heart to leverage that blessing for the Kingdom. Jay truly understands the social, material, spiritual, and technical dilemmas the wealthy face on the way toward a life of fulfillment and generosity.

Bob Buford, Founder, Leadership Network, Author,
Halftime* and *Finishing Well

There are few individuals as passionate, knowledgeable and articulate about the biblical principles on generosity and effective stewardship as Jay Link. The life dilemmas described so clearly by Jay in this book are "real" but seldom addressed. The generous and effective distribution of wealth entrusted to Christians has been stifled by their lack of understanding what dilemmas they face and then not knowing what to do about them. Jay offers clarity on this subject and challenges all of us to be more intentional about our stewardship. This book can result in a "spiritual breakthrough" for those wealthy Christian families desiring to be wise and responsible stewards.

Paul Schultheis, Founder/Senior Managing Partner,
Strategic Resource Group

To Whom Much is Given takes the whole discussion of generous living to a deeper level. Jay puts forward the hard questions we all ask ourselves and provides the context for God-given answers. The last dilemma, "Surrendering All to

Christ", captures the essence of Christian living and should be read often by us all.

**Ken Johns, Tijeras Foundation,
Generous Community Initiative**

The Author

—⁓—

M r. E. G. "Jay" Link has a unique blend of professional experience. He is both an ordained minister as well as a Family Wealth Counselor. Jay has spent decades helping wealthy families develop, implement, and then live out their strategic Master Stewardship Plans allowing them to maximize all that God has entrusted to them. It is his biblical knowledge and professional experience that uniquely qualifies him to authoritatively write, teach, and counsel on biblical stewardship for wealthy Christians.

Jay has personally trained and mentored hundreds of attorneys, accountants, money managers, and financial planners in Family Wealth Counseling for their clients, multiplying his ministry to wealthy families hundreds of times over. His first book, *Family Wealth Counseling: Getting to the Heart of the Matter*, and his Professional Mentoring Program training helped birth a nationwide revolution in wealth transfer planning that has radically changed the way many advisors now work with wealthy families.

Jay has an undying passion for showing wealthy Christian families how to effectively maximize their remaining time, employ their unique talents, and strategically deploy their accumulated treasures to expand and support the Kingdom of God. His family office firm, Kardia, Inc., works exclusively with affluent Christian families to help them develop, implement, and manage their customized, intergenerational Master Stewardship Plans. Its concierge family office approach, unique planning expertise, and Christian worldview make the firm extremely valuable as a long-term resource to the families it serves. With Kardia's hands-on guidance and attentive on-going support, its families are able to effectively and strategically steward all the resources that God has entrusted to them far beyond anything they ever imagined possible.

Acknowledgement

—⟋⟍⟍—

I would like to thank all the wonderful families for whom I have had the honor of serving and counseling through the past several decades. It has been these relationships that have allowed me to learn from their collective lives what I will be sharing with you in this book.

I would particularly like to thank several of our current clients; John Bandimere, Joe Coors, Bob Walker, and Doug and Kristi Dawson for being part of Kardia's advisory team. Their wisdom and encouragement has been invaluable to us. They have also helped us fund several of our "Kingdom impact" initiatives (including this book) to enlighten and encourage other affluent Christian families and their professional advisors on how to successfully navigate the spiritual and financial complexities of possessing wealth.

I would like to thank Russ Minary for continually pushing me to write more books.

I would also like to thank my family, several of my friends and some of our strategic partners who have all offered valuable suggestions to improve the style and content of the book.

But most of all I wish to thank the Lord, for giving me the privilege of playing a very small part in His grand plan for eternity.

Table of Contents

—⁓—

Navigating the *Giving Dilemmas* Affluent Christians Face......73

Introduction

—ᘉ—

What do you do when you have more than enough? Most people only recognize the benefits of having wealth—they focus on the ability to buy new cars and nice clothes, own multiple homes, have bigger and better "toys," experience freedom from worrying about paying bills, saving for retirement, or sending their kids to college. They equate wealth with being able to do whatever they want, whenever they want, and wherever they want.

However, those who have spent their lives amassing assets faster than they thought was possible realize that there is another side to being wealthy. With riches comes responsibility. They are usually the only ones to realize that wealth also brings a host of very serious challenges, difficulties, and dangers. How you use your fortune can build or destroy; it can teach or it can corrupt; it can provide a sense of security or a sense of entitlement. As a wealthy Christian, there comes the realization that what you do with your money has eternal consequences.

I have never met a Christian who did not intellectually accept that all he/she has on this earth belongs to God, and that it has been given out of God's goodness. So, with wealth also comes the increased responsibility of being a good steward (or manager) of both property and finances. We all want to someday hear, "Well done, my good and faithful servant," when we meet Jesus because we had effectively managed the time, talents, and treasures He entrusted to us.

Having spent thousands of hours with Christian families over the past three decades, it has become obvious that they all face the same dilemmas in how to properly steward their possessions—challenges that most people will never confront. I call them "life dilemmas" because they go beyond the basic financial management issues of paying bills, staying out of debt, sticking to a budget, and giving. These dilemmas manifest themselves because of the incredible overflow that God has poured out on some people financially. They are about living with a surplus and leaving a legacy of blessing. They are about managing what God has entrusted to them to use for His purposes and for His Kingdom on the earth—both in and outside of their family.

These ten dilemmas fall into three categories: *Lifestyle Dilemmas, Wealth Transfer Dilemmas, and Giving Dilemmas.* In this book, I will describe each of these ten unique life dilemmas and offer what I hope to be wise and godly counsel to help you successfully navigate these dilemmas in your situation. I hope you find these discussions enlightening and thought-provoking. It is my sincere desire that they will bless you and your family and successfully guide you on your stewardship journey in the years to come.

Navigating the
Lifestyle Dilemmas
Affluent Christians Face

—∾∾—

Navigating Dilemma #1

Should I Just Build Bigger Barns?

—ᵐ—

When your net worth has grown beyond anything you could possibly consume in your lifetime what do you do?

This problem is not new. Jesus addressed this very issue in the parable of the rich farmer.

> *A rich man had a fertile farm that produced fine crops. In fact, his barns were full to overflowing. So he said, "I know! I'll tear down my barns and build bigger ones. Then I'll have room enough to store everything. And I'll sit back and say to myself, 'My friend, you have enough stored away for years to come. Now take it easy! Eat, drink, and be merry!'" But God said to him, "You fool! You will die this very night. Then who will get it all?"*
>
> *Luke 12:16-20* NLT

Families become wealthy when they accumulate more than they choose to consume—not particularly profound, but nonetheless true. Their businesses and/or investments have grown at a much greater rate than their lifestyles. Slowly over the years, they find their "barns" filling up with assets that exceed anything they would have imagined in their younger years.

I remember asking one Christian man if he had any idea when he was twenty that he would one day be worth hundreds of millions of dollars. He chuckled and said, "I had no idea even when I was forty!"

For every "barn builder" there inevitably comes a time when the question must be asked, "Is it time to stop building new and bigger barns to hold my ever-increasing wealth? And if it is, what do I do with all that is still coming in if I do not have any new places to store what we can not use now?"

Here is the rich man's dilemma using a different metaphor, "What do I do when my 'golden goose' continues laying more 'golden eggs' than I can use or store?"

Here is what you do not want to do with your golden goose that produces more golden eggs than you need.

1) Do not kill the goose.

Obviously, a golden goose is a good thing to possess. It is a blessing from God that can take care of your family and your employees. But there may come a point in your life when it might be better to sell the goose, or to turn that goose over to someone else to manage so you no longer have to be tied to its continual daily care and feeding. You might even consider giving the golden goose back to the One who helped you acquire it in the first place. There are many wonderful things that can be done when you have more money than you will ever need. However, the last thing you want to do is end the blessing.

There is a fascinating little book on this subject by the businessman Stanley Tam entitled, *God Owns My Business.*[1] He actually gave his business to the Lord and lived on a very modest salary as an employee of the company. That way the millions of golden eggs that his business laid could *all* be used for Kingdom purposes. I highly recommend reading this book.

2) Do not increase your lifestyle consumption simply because you have an ever-increasing income.

This is very common with many wealthy families. They handle the ever-increasing number of surplus golden eggs being laid by simply continuing to increase their consumption (either consciously or unconsciously). It is very easy to get caught up in what I call the "lifestyle creep"—your consumption continues to rise with your increasing financial capacity. This can happen almost unconsciously over an extended period of time—because you have more, you simply spend more, and because you have more left after that, you never feel like you might be overdoing it.

Over the years we have observed that wealthy families seldom see themselves as being extravagant in their lifestyles (even though most of the rest of the world would view their lifestyles as extraordinarily excessive). The reason is that

---

[1] Tam, Stanley. *God Owns My Business*. New York: Horizon Books, 1991.

they are still spending far less than they actually *could be* spending. For them, *excessive* means "spending more than you can afford to spend" and in that sense they are not excessive. And, honestly, no one on this planet should be acting as anyone else's "lifestyle police." However, if God is blessing you, I do not believe it is because He wants you to consume it all on yourself.

The bottom line question then becomes "How much is enough?" And truthfully, it is not as easy a question to answer as some might think.

I remember some years ago a wealthy gentleman asked me that same question in these words, "How much do you think we ought to be living on?"

I answered him, "That is a very good question and one you should be asking, but you are asking the wrong person. You need to ask the Owner how much of *His* wealth *He* thinks you should be living on."

If we understand and accept that we are merely stewards (managers) of God's possessions and not the owners, these issues become much clearer. We should be consulting with the Owner on what He wants done with *His* stuff.

God always blesses us so that we can be a blessing to others. This has been true since God's first dealings with Abraham:

I will bless you,
And make your name great. . . .
And in you all the families of the earth will be
blessed.

Genesis 12:2-3

I like to ask people this question, "Are you living like a bucket or a pipe?" It may seem to be an odd metaphorical question, but the point of the question is this: "Are God's blessings merely filling up your life to overflowing, or are His blessings flowing through you to build His Kingdom and to help others?" A bucket is designed to hold things (liquids, dirt, etc.). A pipe is designed to pass things through to another location (fluids, air, etc.). The bucket holds what it receives and the pipe transfers on what it receives. So, in regards to the wealth that God has so graciously entrusted to you, let me ask, "Are you living your life like a bucket or a pipe? Are you just storing up what you receive or are you passing it on?"

3) Do not keep piling the excess up in bigger and bigger barns without a strategy for what to do with it.

This was the mistake of the rich farmer. He obviously had no plans to dispose of the excess from his golden goose (his farm). And he apparently had no plans to increase his lifestyle to consume the surplus either. His problem was that he had no other vision than to build bigger barns and retire. The rich farmer did not necessarily make a mistake in building bigger barns, but for him, the building of bigger barns became the end in and of itself.

That is why Jesus called him a fool. The farmer already had more than enough and had no greater purpose for his increasing wealth than storing it away where it would benefit no one. He missed God's bigger purpose for why he was being blessed in the first place—he thought it was just for him, but in reality it was so that he could be a blessing to others. He made the careless mistake of not having a plan for what to do with his wealth beyond letting it pile up.

Herein lies the dilemma: "What does God want me to do with my ever-increasing surplus wealth?" Too many never come to realize that what they have is already more than they will ever need, and they therefore simply store it away until they die.

In fact, a family will never be able to determine how much of their accumulated wealth is actually surplus until they know how to answer these two foundational questions:

1) "How much is enough for us to maintain our present lifestyle?"
2) "How much is enough to leave our loved ones as an inheritance?"

These are not easy questions to answer. In my years of counseling wealthy Christian families, I have found no two answers exactly the same. You see, your blessing of more than enough is very much tied to your calling to be a blessing here on earth—your calling to help see the Kingdom of God expanded. It has to do with what God's purpose is for your life. The challenge is to be listening carefully enough to discern His call.

These questions also cannot be adequately answered in a vacuum. Your material blessings are part of a unique partnership between you and God. He wants to spend time with you communicating His plans for these possessions. This is why developing a comprehensive Master Stewardship Plan—a plan that uniquely fits your family's situation and calling— is critically important to achieving a God-led course of action for you and your family and how you will seek to impact His Kingdom.

You see, you can choose to live your life one of two ways. Either you live your life on purpose or you live your life by accident. In other words, you can plan your life and live your plan or you can simply let the flow of life-events and circumstances sweep you down the river of time taking you wherever it will. The latter—living by accident—is sadly the way most people live their lives. It is the way the rich farmer lived his life. God, however, created us to live our lives on purpose. (See Ephesians 5:15-16, Psalm 90:12a.)[2]

Unfortunately, when it comes to building one's financial "empire" we can often find ourselves doing it without any real divine purpose behind it. Successful people continue to build up their "pile of stuff" because they have become exceedingly good at what they do. They also find great emotional enjoyment and personal satisfaction in building, so they keep on building.

However, I think there is a foundational question that we, as believers, need to ask ourselves, "What is my purpose for continuing to build my financial empire when my pile of stuff is already higher than I will ever need it to be?" Jesus tells us plainly that accumulating excess wealth as a sole end in itself is entirely futile. Jesus states, *"For what will it profit a man if he gains the whole world and forfeits his soul?"* (Matthew 16:26).

---

[2] For more on "Are You Living Your Life on Purpose or by Accident?" see my book, *Spiritual Thoughts on Material Things*.

Paul addresses this issue in 1 Corinthians 3:12-15 when he says,

Now if any man builds on the foundation with gold, silver, precious stones, wood, hay, straw, each man's work will become evident; for the day will show it because it is to be revealed with fire, and the fire itself will test the quality of each man's work. If any man's work which he has built on it remains, he will receive a reward. If any man's work is burned up, he will suffer loss; but he himself will be saved, yet so as through fire.

May I ask, "What foundation are you building on? What materials are you building with? And *why* are you building what you are building?"

You can see why this first stewardship dilemma can be daunting for wealthy families. It takes some time and soul searching to solve, but it is worth the time and effort. Failure to resolve this dilemma may lead you to the same end as the rich farmer in Jesus' parable. For a lack of a better plan, you will keep piling up your wealth for no good reason—until it is too late!

Navigating Dilemma #2

It's Lonely at the Top

—ɷ—

Clichés become well known because they have a strong element of truth in them. And the old cliché, "It's lonely at the top" is no exception. It does not even matter what you are at the top of, the population there is always very sparse. This is equally true with people whom the Lord has blessed with material prosperity. The more prosperous people become, the fewer close and intimate relationships they will have.

Some years ago, I was sharing this thought with a wealthy couple in their early fifties. The husband interrupted me and with a look of epiphany on his face, turned to his wife, and said, "You know, I never saw it until now, but when we were young, just getting started in business and were struggling to make ends meet, we had all kinds of close, intimate friends. Over the years, however, as we have become more and more successful, our number of friends has grown smaller and smaller, until right now I can honestly say I don't think we have any close friends that we spend time with anymore."

As this couple's material lifestyle increased, their relational lifestyle diminished proportionately. The more earthly wealth they had, the smaller their circle of friends.

The accumulation of wealth separates those who possess it from those who do not. This is sad, but all too common. There truly is a divide between the "Haves" and the "Have Nots."

However, if you understand some of the reasons for this, you can then do something about it. As Christians, we need to not only be stewards of our worldly wealth, but also our eternal wealth. Relationships are one thing we will be able to take with us to heaven.

The Barriers Wealth Builds

There are five barriers that separate those who have wealth from those who do not. I will briefly touch on each of them and then offer some suggestions on what the "Haves" can do to be good stewards of their relationships with the "Have Nots" of the world.

(1) The first barrier to relationships between the "Haves" and the "Have Nots" is a prejudice the "Have Nots" feel towards the "Haves" that I call *"wealthism." Wealthism* causes people to think, "With all your money how can you possibly have any problems? I mean you have a beautiful home, three new cars, nice clothes, money in the bank, and a great income. You can buy whatever you want and go wherever you want, whenever you want. How dare you complain about anything! If I had that kind of wealth you would never hear me complaining!"

Regardless of what having wealth does, it does not make anyone more than human, and as a human being, we will always face problems in this world. It would come as a substantial surprise to the "Have Nots" that the "Haves" still deal with a myriad of personal issues in their lives—many of them the same as the "Have Nots" face, and several other problems directly caused by the burdens and responsibilities of possessing great wealth.

One of the greatest deceptions of the evil one is the mistaken notion that money makes you happy and the more money you have the happier you will be. (After all, *"Money is the answer to everything"* [Ecclesiastes 10:19], right?) Because of the "Have Nots'" attitude of *wealthism*, the "Haves" cannot be real and honest with them about their pain, their problems, their struggles, and their temptations— the "Have Nots" simply cannot relate to or appreciate that they could actually have any legitimate problems.

(2) The second barrier to relationships between these two groups is that *wealth intimidates.* We have all seen it and felt it. I would venture to say that without exception every one of us, to one degree or another, would be intimidated if Bill Gates, one of the richest men in the world, were to walk into a room and come over to talk to us.

I remember years ago, a very wealthy man (worth about $15 million) wanted to introduce me to an even wealthier man (worth about $150 million). I will never forget what the man of lesser wealth confessed to me. He said, "Compared to him, I'm small potatoes." I wondered if he knew how many people thought that same thing about him?

From his comment, it was obvious that even though he was worth a considerable $15 million, he was still intimidated by a man who was worth $150 million. Wealth intimidates, and the more of it you have, the more intimidating you will be to others below your net worth.

We do not have a caste system in our culture like many other countries, but we do have clear class distinctions that are very emotional. And this emotional class warfare can be seen nowhere more clearly than in the hostile rhetoric of politicians who are frequently characterizing the "Haves" as the enemy of the "Have Nots."

(3) The third barrier is that *wealth creates one-sided relationships*. If a "Have" and a "Have Not" sit down for a meal in a restaurant, who will most often pay the bill? Regardless of the occasion, there is usually an assumption on everyone's part that Mr. "Have" will pick up the tab—or buy the tickets for the movie or whatever else it might be.

What is interesting is that this sense of obligation may be more real in the minds of the Mr. or Mrs. "Have" than in the minds of the "Have Nots." There seems to be a sense of duty to pick up the tab since they are the ones who can most easily afford it. All of you who are "Haves" know exactly what I am talking about.

If Mr. and Mrs. "Have Not" want to do something to show the "Haves" their appreciation for a kindness given, there is a difficult question to ask, "What do you get the man and woman who already have everything, or at least have everything they want?" Well, for the "Have Nots," this is a serious problem which makes their relationship seem one-sided. This economic disparity prevents them from being able to relate as equals, and thus friends.

(4) The fourth barrier to relationships between these two groups is that *wealth bestows power*. The old cliché, "He who has the gold makes the rules" is all too true in our society today. Power comes by default with wealth. Everyone is eager to please the rich.

Unfortunately, this also means that the "Haves" too often use their wealth as a substitute for personal interaction. For example, when Mr. "Have Not" needs to paint his house, he may call several of his friends over to help him. Mr. "Have," on the other hand, will just call a painter (who is likely a stranger) to do the same job for him because he can afford to pay to have the work done. In the end, the job is taken care of with a minimum of personal interaction for Mr. "Have." He has the power and money to buy the needed work relationships allowing him to bypass a great deal of personal interaction with other people. The "Haves" will often use their wealth to solve problems instead of getting other people involved. They "buy" a solution, minus any real personal investment. People know that when Mr. "Have" speaks, everyone listens!

However, if Mr. "Have" were to call some of the "Have Nots" to come help him paint his house, the "Have Nots" would likely feel taken advantage of unless they were paid. Can you not just hear them after they leave? "I mean, after all, if he can afford to hire someone to paint his house; why is he imposing on us to do it for free?" Again, the "Have's" wealth hinders friendships from developing.

(5) The fifth barrier to these relationships is that *wealth needs to be protected.* The "Haves," out of both fear and necessity, need to build either literal or figurative walls around themselves and the things they own. They require more locks and alarm systems than the "Have Nots" because they have more stuff that needs to be protected. Yet, tragically, in their appropriate efforts to protect their possessions, the "Haves" inadvertently end up building walls that keep the "Have Nots" out of their lives. Not only have they physically—and possibly emotionally—walled the "Have Nots" *out*, they have also walled themselves *in*.

Breaking Down Those Barriers

While completely eliminating these barriers is impossible, an odd thing happens when "Haves" and "Have Nots" catch a similar vision in addressing some local concern or social ministry. It is different when they get together to paint a room for a disabled veterans' home or an orphanage. It is different when they stand side by side serving food at a homeless shelter or at a community picnic for single parent families. It is different when they are elbow-to-elbow tutoring underprivileged youth. It is also different when "Haves" turn their wealth into something that makes a difference in their community rather than remaining a social wall. Suspicion turns to gratitude, and one-sided relationships turn into partnerships.[3]

---

[3] For more on *"Breaking Down Those Barriers,"* see chapter 16, "Building Bridges Instead of Walls," in my book *Family Wealth Counseling: Getting to the Heart of the Matter.*

Suddenly it is not about telling each other your problems, but discussing how to solve bigger issues for others. A person with expertise in building a business is no longer regarded as someone out to make a buck off of others, but is regarded as a respected advisor helping a charitable organization grow and become more effective and efficient. The dividing barriers no longer matter as they join together in a God-given purpose reaching out to their communities and the world.

Families need guidance in determining how their excess wealth can be used to help others and accomplish the things God has put on their hearts. This is one important key to tearing down relationship barriers making the remainder of your life far more fulfilling and rewarding than if you stayed behind your walls of protection.

Navigating Dilemma #3

Everyone Is Trying
to Sell Me Something,
So Who Can I Trust?

—ⱱⱱ—

E very professional wants to work with the wealthy. That
is certainly the prevailing thinking in the financial
services industry.

Because of this focused attention, this collective group of
well-to-do people has become the target market of virtually
any professional that has something to sell. The group has
even been given a specific name by marketers: the "affluent
market." Many books have been written and many confer-
ences held expressly to help advisors access this narrow, but
very desirable cross-section of our population.

It should come as no surprise to anyone, then, that people
of wealth are constantly bombarded with offers for "hot"
new financial products, innovative planning tools, or state-
of-the-art services. It is hard for them to turn around or meet
someone new without hearing a sales pitch of some kind.

With this ever-constant intrusion of professionals
hawking their wares, these affluent "targets" grow more and

more skeptical about anyone and everyone who approaches them with another "opportunity" to improve their current situation with the latest and greatest whatever. Those financial advisors who seek to work with the wealthy will all say that the hardest part of getting a wealthy client is just getting in front of them in the first place. Out of necessity and to maintain sanity, the wealthy have made themselves extremely inaccessible.

One of the most common complaints we hear from people about past "marketing presentations" they have endured is that it seems the presenters have some private agenda or pet product to promote. The fear is that their advice might be skewed because of an obvious conflict of interest between doing what is in the client's best interest and selling them something that is in the advisor's best interest—be it life insurance, money management services, trust services, legal services, etc.—and it is usually a "one-size-fits-all" product. Everything else they offer to do for a client is nothing more than "window dressing" to enable them to make that sale.

In a study conducted by Russ Prince, wealthy individuals were asked how ethical they felt various advisors were in their practices. It is interesting that those who sold products were viewed as being the least ethical, while those who charged fees with no product sales were considered the most ethical. Accountants were considered the most ethical, fee-based advisors of all.

But with the merging of so many industries, we are seeing more and more accountants and attorneys who now also sell financial and investment products along with their customary professional services. The waters of objectivity are muddier than ever.

It is not that someone who sells a product or service is necessarily unethical, but they are often perceived to be. Thus this perception is an automatic strike against any advisor coming to them who is not practicing strictly on a fee basis. There is an automatic negative slant against the objectivity of the advisor, regardless of the actual character of that person or the value of whatever they may have to sell.

Then, of course, you have advisors who are very narrow in their focus of services. They have a pet product, tool, or service they offer and that is really all they do. How this product or service might fit into an integrated, overall master plan is well beyond what such advisors offer. The "have I got the perfect product for you" pitch sounds a lot like the fictitious insurance agent who always started his conversations with, "Life insurance is the answer, now what is your question?"

I have even had an estate-planning attorney tell me, "We recommend limited partnerships to all our clients." Oh, really—*all of them*? No matter who they are, what they have, or what they want to do? Everyone gets one? This kind of "one-trick-pony" planning is all too common, and it only feeds the perceived conflicts of interest with advisors. The wealthy person often wonders, "Am I getting customized advice or boilerplate planning?"

Whether the conflict of interest is real or perceived makes little difference. As the saying goes, "Perception is reality." Why enter into a working relationship with an advisor you are not sure you can trust? You must find a way to evaluate if the advisor really has your best interest in mind and whether he is offering you more than just an "off-the-shelf" plan with some hidden, ulterior motive.

So, in a word, the bottom line is *trust*. How can you know who you can trust to give you objective and sound counsel in planning? How can you know the person you are meeting with shares your basic values and worldview? You are giving this person sway over what you do with millions of dollars that you have worked so hard to accumulate. Will they focus this planning in a way that reflects how you think, or will they find a way to highjack it to support *their* values instead, even though they are contradictory to yours? Are you going to work with an advisor who has a common biblical worldview and has integrated that worldview into his practice or are you going to work with an advisor who neither knows your God nor His Word basing his advice on a secular and worldly perspective?

In addition, many wealthy Christian families are never even introduced to several planning options simply because their advisors live and advise from a different point of view. The advisors may be good at what they do and have great recommendations from other clients, but because of their different worldview, they never offer to do for their clients what their clients might choose to do if they really knew all the available options.

Let me give you an example. In estate planning, most advisors will minimize charitable giving in lieu of increasing the amount going to the heirs, even though it might mean a large part of the estate will go to the government in taxes instead of worthy causes that honor Christ and expand

His Kingdom. Because they do not value building God's Kingdom as you do, Kingdom-building planning options for your wealth are never even discussed. This is not a conflict of interest as much as it is a difference in thinking—even if the advisors are Christians, they may still be thinking and counseling from a secular worldview. If it is not something the advisor values, why would he or she ever even ask you if that is what you would like to do with your wealth?

Secular advisors will always ask a different set of questions and come up with a different plan than someone who is operating from a biblical worldview—always. Look at the chart below to see a real example of how a secular firm offered a more traditional plan to a wealthy family suggesting it was superior.

Beneficiaries	**Creative Plan**	**Traditional Plan**
Kingdom	$17 million	$ 7 million
IRS	$ 0	$ 9 million
Children	$12 million	$13 million

Note that for the sake of giving a total of $1 million more to their five kids, the advisors were willing to take $10 million away from Kingdom giving and give ninety percent of that money to the IRS. For most people with a secular worldview, this might make sense, but is that the best stewardship distribution option for a Christian family seeking to see real positive Kingdom change in the world?

On more than one occasion I have had secular advisors tell me that it is irrelevant whether the money goes to charity or to the government in taxes because neither directly benefits the family. I could not disagree more. The positive impact on a family, when giving millions of dollars away to worthy Christian organizations and causes is infinitely more beneficial to a family (emotionally and spiritually) than paying that same amount to the Federal Government in unnecessary taxes, which nobody feels good about. The secular worldview focuses only on "me and mine." If something has to go to others, then it does not really matter where it goes.[4]

I would estimate that over eighty percent of Christians have made no provision for Kingdom giving. For those few who have, the amount of that giving compared to their net worth was merely a token gesture.

I am convinced it is not that these Christians are not interested in giving, it is because their secular advisors are not asking them the right questions. The fact is, an advisor with a contradictory worldview cannot ask the right questions and consequently a believer will never come to discover the right answers.

The following is a checklist of questions to ask a potential advisor to help minimize the risk of getting into a professional relationship with a planner who may not be best for you:

1) How many years have you been doing what you are proposing to do for us?
2) How many families are you currently doing advanced, estate planning for annually?
3) How many families have you worked with who have a net worth equal to or higher than ours?

---

[4] For more on "Are Your Advisors Asking You the Right Questions?" see my book, *Spiritual Thoughts on Material Things*.

4) May we talk with three families for whom you have implemented plans?

5) May we see a complete, written, sample plan of the work that you have done for other clients like us?

6) How much time do you devote to getting to know us and our situation before you start the planning?

7) How long will it take to go through your planning process?

8) Do you work with our existing advisors or will we work with you in place of our current advisors?

9) How much personal time will you spend with us in the planning process?

10) How do you get paid?

11) Is your planning process overtly Christian? Do you operate using a biblical worldview in your planning?

12) What has been your personal spiritual pilgrimage? Can you give me a reference of a Pastor/Elder in your church who I can ask about your involvement and level of spiritual maturity?

13) Will you conduct family meetings to help us communicate our plans to our heirs and help us prepare them for their inheritance?

14) Once the plan you design for us is implemented, what are your on-going services to help us keep the plan fully operational?

15) How do you handle future (life or financial) changes that will require maintenance on or modifications to our plan?

Even more important than all of these questions—even though it is the most subjective evaluation of all—listen to the Holy Spirit. If you or your spouse is not entirely at peace with moving forward in a relationship with an advisor, do not do it—even if you do not know why. Colossians 3:15 tells us, "*Let the peace of Christ rule in your hearts.*" That word *rule* can also be translated "be the umpire." God gives us His peace to know when we are "safe" to go on with a plan, or takes it away when we should be telling someone or something in our lives, "No thank you!"

Let me make one final comment about conflicts of interest. We all face conflicts of interest almost every day of our lives. It is impossible, in my judgment, to be in any kind of business and avoid all potential conflicts of interest all the time. So the real issue is not so much, "Does this advisor have a conflict of interest?" but "Would this advisor do what is best for me even if it is not best for him?" You should be confident that the advisor's personal character is solid enough that when tempted to overlook your best interest for his own, he would have little difficulty being open about it and advising what is best for you.

Highly skilled advisors who are men and women of the highest levels of personal integrity are available, but finding them can feel like searching for the proverbial "needle in a haystack." It is a dilemma for wealthy families, but the benefits of taking the time to find the right advisors will pay huge dividends for you and your family in the long run. It is one more challenge inherent in being a good steward of the abundance God has entrusted to you.

Navigating the
Wealth Transfer Dilemmas
Affluent Christians Face

—∽—

Navigating Dilemma #4

Blessing (and Not Cursing)
the Next Generation

—⁓—

The single most difficult planning challenge for the affluent centers around this complex question: "How much of our wealth should we leave to our heirs?"

This has been a troubling dilemma that has nagged at wealthy parents for millennia. Even King Solomon (possibly the richest and the wisest man who has ever lived) struggled to answer this for himself. In Ecclesiastes 2:18-19, 21 NIV Solomon laments,

> *I hated all the things I had toiled for under the sun,*
> *because I must leave them to the one who comes after*
> *me, and who knows whether he will be a wise man*
> *or a fool? Yet he will have control over all the work*
> *into which I have poured my effort and skill under*
> *the sun. This too is meaningless. . . . For a man may*
> *do his work with wisdom, knowledge and skill, and*
> *then he must leave all he owns to someone who has*

not worked for it. This too is meaningless and a great misfortune.

Affluent parents innately know that wealth is dangerous. Like a blazing fire, it can cook and warm (good) or it can burn and destroy (bad). Which it will do for their heirs depends to a great extent on how effectively they hand this "fire" off to them.

There are real and serious dangers to heirs who gain excessive access to unearned wealth. The wealth that parents leave their heirs is meant to bless, but it can and often does, curse instead.

Jessie O'Neill's excellent book, *The Golden Ghetto*[5] gives us five "bitter fruits" that can manifest themselves in heirs who have been given unearned riches. Let me introduce them to you and then briefly comment on each.

Bitter Fruit #1
Lack of Motivation to Work

When an heir has all the money he or she needs, what motivation is there to go out and get a job or do something meaningful with their life?

Some years ago, I was discussing this issue with a wealthy mother and she said she understood this problem all too well. She had been chiding her high school son to buckle down and start getting better grades so he could get into a good college, get a good education, and get a good job. Her son responded, "I don't need to get good grades in high

---

[5] O'Neill, Jessie H. *The Golden Ghetto: The Psychology of Affluence.* Center City, MN: Hazelden, 1997.

school or college, because I don't need to get a good job, because when I turn twenty-two, I get the money in the trust that Grandma set up for me."

Whether it seems like it or not, all of us need that proverbial "carrot on the end of the stick" motivating us to go out and earn our own way in the world. It lets us know that we are capable human beings who can add some value to the world God has placed us in. Although everyone dreams about how nice it would be to have all of our material comforts provided for freely, only the wealthy know the downside of actually experiencing that and losing sight of living for any larger purpose than just pleasing ourselves. Many wealthy families—especially if they are first generation wealthy—rob their children of a life without even knowing it by taking away their need and motivation to work by leaving them too much of an inheritance.

Bitter Fruit #2
Lack of Perseverance

When people have plenty of financial resources, they do not have to endure hardship. They can simply bail out and go on to other things or just throw money at problems to make them go away. They do not appreciate the money going out because they never worked to earn it in the first place. If they want something, they can buy the best of whatever it is they want. They do not need to work hard at anything, or persevere through difficult circumstances to resolve them. Thus they only reach a certain level of discomfort in any situation before running away, and with enough money, they can be running away their entire lives.

Bitter Fruit #3
Problems with Relationships

This is one of the most bitter of all fruits. Consider the exposure unplanned wealth can create for heirs. All of a sudden your heirs are wealthy. How can they know whether people are genuinely interested in them or merely interested in enjoying the benefits of their wealth? Remember, the wealthy will always have many "friends." (See Proverbs 19:4.) An heir may eventually begin to question, "Do you love me or my money?"

Bitter Fruit #4
Self-Worth Struggles

One of the main ways we build positive self-images for ourselves is by what we accomplish. Working to get a good grade, practicing hard to be a starter on a sports team, building something with our hands, becoming a member of an honor society—whatever it may be that we accomplish in life—all contribute to building a positive self-worth.

But what if your greatest accomplishment is that you just happened to be born into a wealthy family? If that is the case, kids often struggle to know if they really are able to accomplish anything on their own without the backing of the family money, name, reputation, or influence. That silver spoon they are born with can be great for taking care of basic physical needs. However, it can be a stumbling block to persevering through the struggles and character building challenges that come with not having everything you need easily provided. It is simply not true that having everything a person wants can give them a healthy self-esteem.

Bitter Fruit #5
Poor Understanding and
Managing of Finances

A child will never learn to manage money well if he can never run out of it. He does not need to get on a budget. He does not need to learn to invest wisely. He does not need to know how to save up for something he has been dreaming of getting. And because of that, when he does get what he has asked for, he seldom appreciates it. Even what he gives to others means little because he did nothing to earn what he gave away.

Such heirs risk becoming obsessed with self-consumption. Their whole world can begin to revolve around their individual wants, turning them into the well-known and little-regarded "spoiled, rich kid." And, the younger an heir is when they receive their unearned inheritance, the greater the chance of this outcome.

Leaving Good Fruit to Your Heirs

I like what the billionaire investor, Warren Buffet, said about his inheritance plans for his loved ones. He said, "I want to give my children enough of an inheritance that they feel like they can do anything, but not so much of an inheritance that they may choose to do nothing." What Warren Buffet is really saying is that he wants to fund *life-opportunities* for his heirs, but not *lifestyle*. (And there is a huge difference in the amount of an inheritance depending on which of these you choose.) When I share Buffett's statement with our Christian parents, they universally nod their heads in agreement.

If this then is a valid guideline, we must attempt to determine what would be the level of inheritance that will allow them to feel like they can do anything—and the level of inheritance that might de-motivate them from developing meaningful and productive lives. Within these parameters, we can create a broad philosophical starting point with which to begin our decision making about how much to leave each person and the best ways to leave it.

I remember a man once said to me, "I do not know what to do about an inheritance for my son. He is such a fool."

I told him, "If that is indeed the case, then the answer is very simple. Solomon tells us in Proverbs 19:10a NIV that, '*It is not fitting for a fool to live in luxury.*' He goes on to say in Proverbs 17:16 NIV, '*Of what use is money in the hand of a fool, since he has no desire to get wisdom?*'"

I added, "If your son is indeed an incurable fool, then let him be a poor fool, do not make him a rich one."

But the definitive word in my statement is *incurable*. The traditional planning process sees a problem with an heir and attempts to address it by putting a bandage on it (i.e. if a child cannot handle money, their inheritance would be put into a trust with a spendthrift provision to keep them from wasting it all). A superior approach is to first seek to solve the child's foolish attitudes and behaviors. Much of this can happen even before you leave them anything. This can be a great opportunity to work on your relationship with your child to more fully enjoy the time you have now.

In other words, if a son is bad at handling money, we help dad invest the time and set up the opportunities while he is still here to help his son learn how to better handle money. Just because he is your son does not mean that he has your knowledge, experience, or your natural aptitude in these areas.

The first planning objective should be for parents to equip their heirs with the needed wisdom regarding how to properly and effectively handle their inheritance, however much you might choose that to be. Solomon said in Ecclesiastes 7:11-12a,

Wisdom along with an inheritance is good and an advantage to those who see the sun. For wisdom is protection just as money is protection.

Parent's planning mantra should be, "If we are going to leave our heirs wealth, let us also leave them the wisdom to know what to do with it." If you are not going to give them both, do not give them either. If you give them the wealth without the wisdom, the blazing fire of wealth is going to burn and destroy them—it will be a curse and not a blessing.

To help assess how well your offspring are exercising wisdom, let me suggest these four Maturity Markers. They will give you a hands-on and practical way to proactively address and work to correct any problem areas in your heirs' lives.

Spiritual Maturity Marker #1
(An Heir's Relationship with God)

Signs for this Spiritual Maturity Marker would include an heir who is...
 (1) growing as a personal follower of Jesus;
 (2) developing in godly character; and
 (3) ministering to others.

Emotional Maturity Marker #2
(An Heir's Relationship with Himself)

Signs for this Emotional Maturity Marker would include an heir who is...
 (1) taking responsibility for his/her actions and proactively seeking to correct his/her mistakes and sins;
 (2) controlling his/her anger, frustration, disappointment, and stress appropriately; and
 (3) avoiding chronic problematic and self-destructive behavior.

Relational Maturity Marker #3
(An Heir's Relationship with Others)

Signs for this Relational Maturity Marker would include an heir who is...

(1) developing and maintaining healthy and meaningful long-term relationships with friends and family;

(2) treating other people with respect and dignity; and

(3) making personal sacrifices for the benefit of others.

Financial Maturity Marker #4 (An Heir's Relationship with Money)

Signs for this Financial Maturity Marker would include an heir who is...

(1) living financially independent of parents;

(2) exercising consumptive self-control in spending; and

(3) engaging in enthusiastic and generous giving.

A Place to Start

These maturity markers should better equip you to have real, meaningful dialog with your children enabling you to establish measurable and attainable standards by which to make more objective inheritance decisions instead of having those decisions driven primarily by emotion and guilt.[6]

That is why we strongly believe that the solution to this inheritance dilemma will be achieved far more effectively by what you do in your living room with your family than by what you do in some conference room with your lawyers and advisors. It is far more important how you prepare your

---

[6] For more on matters to consider before choosing how much inheritance to give to each heir, see my books, *Spiritual Thoughts on Material Things* and *Family Wealth Counseling: Getting to the Heart of the Matter.*

heirs than how you prepare your legal documents. And that is why having open and honest family meetings—bringing the heirs into the planning process so they can know what is happening and why—is so critically important.

Start now, while Mom and Dad (or Grandma and Grandpa) are still alive. Begin the mentoring process of preparing the next generations for what will be coming. We are convinced that personally revealing your plans to your heirs in an organized and thoughtful way before you relocate to heaven is vastly more effective in successfully transferring wealth to the next generation than having some attorney reveal your plans to them after your funeral. Does that not really make more sense?

Navigating Dilemma #5

Getting Off the Business Merry-Go-Round Safely

—ɷ—

Successful business people will end up investing most of their adult working lives building their companies. They typically devote fifty to sixty hours a week, year after year, continually constructing, enhancing, and reinventing their businesses into finely-tuned machines. The successes of their companies are seen in both their ever-increasing annual profits as well as their ever-increasing fair market value. Figuring out how to make a business bigger and better is part of the fun. And these fiercely independent, entrepreneurial risk-takers have demonstrated that they are very good at it.

An owner's "fingerprints" are all over his business. And in many cases, even after decades, the owner remains the central cog in the on-going operation of his business machine. With his lifetime investment of 50,000 or more hours, he has become the consummate expert in his field. No other single area has consumed a larger portion of his life than his business.

Even though Christians would readily acknowledge that it has been by the Lord's providence and blessing their businesses have succeeded—as Deuteronomy 8:18 says, *"for it is He* [God] *who is giving you power to make wealth, that He may confirm His covenant"*—by the sheer amount of time they have invested, much of their identity is wrapped up in what they have built. These business builders, without exception, have a compelling desire to see what they have built continue even after they are no longer around to watch over it.

Herein is another life dilemma that wealthy Christians face. They ponder, "Now that I have built this well running 'merry-go-round,' how do I now get off without hurting myself, my family or the business in the process?" In other words, "What should I do with the 'golden goose' that the Lord has blessed me with when I am no longer willing or able to continue to care for it?"

This is no small matter. Retirement is easy when you are working in someone else's business. You simply announce your retirement, attend the retirement dinner, accept the gold watch, and go enjoy the rest of your life. It is the owner's problem to figure out how to replace you. But when it is your business, your retirement—and even more importantly your death—it can create gaping holes in the company that cannot and will not be effectively filled without tremendous forethought and strategic planning.

In a very real sense, the business that has given you so much freedom during your lifetime also, in many ways, holds you as its prisoner. You may own it, but it also owns you!

The business succession planning challenge is further compounded if you wish to keep your family business in the family—because the "gene-pool" you have to draw upon for your successor is exceedingly limited. And just because your heirs may have much of the same DNA as you, it does not mean that God has built within them the same combination of talents, passions, and calling for your business as He did in you.

In fact, it is exceedingly rare when He creates a carbon copy of a parent in one of the children. And even if He did, it will still take that child many years in the business to gain the experience and the knowledge that multiple decades of devotion to the business have afforded you as you built it from the ground up.

Now, as if all this was not enough to make this daunting life dilemma overwhelming, you need to add to this the legal and tax aspects of getting your golden goose to your successor(s) without being devastated by capital gains or gift/estate taxes.

It is not enough to figure out *who* is going to take your place in the business, you also need to figure out *how* to get it to them in a tax efficient manner so you do not end up having to sell—or gut—the golden goose to come up with the cash to pay the taxes on the transfer.

A Christian gentleman who is a member of a nationally known family was forced to take their family-owned business public in order to raise the funds necessary to pay the estate taxes on its transfer to the next generation. In other words, they had to sell the business in order to keep it. Yet, they were not even able to keep a controlling percentage of the shares of the company within their family. This lack of strategic planning rendered the family to be nothing more than minority stockholders of a publicly-traded company that their father used to own. They lost their family business because they failed to effectively address this dilemma.

There are no quick fixes or simple answers to the transfer dilemma. And the less time one has until he or she hands the business "mantle" over to someone else, the more urgent and daunting the task becomes.

As a steward of the business that God has entrusted to you, the only option that is *not* available to you is *to do nothing*—to simply ignore the situation because it is problematic. Why not finish the business of your business with the same intensity and creativity that you used all those years to build it?

Let me give you an example of a successful transfer.

Keeping the Family Business in the Family

Tom Durant was a young man when he began a manufacturing business in Nashville, Tennessee. Almost from the start he experienced one major expansion after another that would ultimately multiply his company's size a hundred times over. His trust in God in regards to taking some calculated risks, along with his skillful management paid off "in spades" for his wife Sandy and him. They had become multi-millionaires.

As Durant Manufacturing, Inc. ballooned into a multi-million-dollar business, Tom faced several new problems and challenges. First, the huge success of his business had catapulted him into the maximum estate tax bracket. Second, only one of his four sons was actively involved in the business. Tom and Sandy wanted this one son, Jim, to inherit the business. Since the company represented the vast majority of their estate, they wanted to pass the company on to him, while still providing an equal inheritance to their other three boys.

Tom and Sandy realized that if they sold the business outright to Jim, they would lose fifteen percent of the value of the business to capital gains taxes. If they waited to pass the business on to Jim after they go to be with Jesus, their estate would be facing up to a forty-nine percent shrinkage due to estate taxes—undoubtedly leading to the forced liquidation of the company to pay the taxes. Tom and Sandy had no idea how to solve these problems and because of that, like so many people, they had done nothing at all about it.

A Creative Solution

Through a very sophisticated wealth transfer planning technique, Tom and Sandy solved their capital gains and estate tax problems and achieved all their business, personal, and charitable goals. The first step was for Tom to gift outright one percent of his C-corp. stock to Jim. Tom now owned ninety-nine percent of the stock and his son Jim owned one percent.

Then, Tom began an annual gifting program of one-fifteenth of his stock to a Charitable Remainder Unitrust (CRUT) for the next fifteen years until all his stock had been gifted to the CRUT. Each year as he made the partial transfer,

Tom and Sandy received a substantial current income tax deduction. The corporation, using the increased cash flow now available due to Tom's semi-retirement, offered to buy the stock from the CRUT each year as it was gifted. Once purchased, the corporation simply retired the redeemed stock as treasury stock. As these annual transfers to the CRUT and buy-backs occurred, Jim's small initial percentage of ownership in the company continued to increase each year as less and less stock was outstanding. Ultimately, after the fifteenth year, Jim owned all outstanding shares of Durant Manufacturing stock, making him one hundred percent owner of the company. Through this process, they effectively transferred the entire company to Jim, capital gains and estate tax free.

This process solved the transfer tax problem; however, the Durants still did not know what to do about providing an equal inheritance to all four children. First, the total amount the other three children would have to inherit in order to equal the value of the business that Jim would receive was calculated. That total amount became the figure that was used for the amount of the survivorship life insurance contract that Tom and Sandy would place inside their children's Wealth Replacement Trust (the IRS calls that an "Irrevocable Life Insurance Trust"). Now the other three sons would receive their equal inheritance from the Wealth Replacement Trust and the other estate assets would pass, tax-free, to them using the Durants' lifetime exclusions.

The Durants, using a portion of their CRUT income, as well as the tax savings from making the transfers to the CRUT, made tax-free gifts to fund their children's Wealth

Replacement Trust using their annual gift exclusions. With this plan, Jim got the business and the other three sons got an equal amount of cash along with other estate assets. Everyone was happy.

A Kingdom Benefit

This, however, was not the end of the story. This plan produced a massive sum of money that was now on its way to support Kingdom causes. When Tom and Sandy first thought about what they might like to do with these newly created millions of charitable funds, they were really rather at a loss to know where to give it all. They began praying that the Holy Spirit would give them guidance on how to be the best possible stewards of this substantial fortune. After a few more months, they developed a Master Stewardship Plan that included an overall strategy to underwrite some very exciting projects with seven different ministries. They created a public family foundation and made plans to provide these ministries with hundreds of thousands of dollars of annual support from their foundation endowment funds.

Not only did the Durants accomplish all their personal and family goals and objectives with their Master Stewardship Plan, but in the process of taking care of themselves and their family, they were also able to create a major endowment to continue to support the seven Christian ministries into perpetuity. You can almost hear God saying to the Durants, "Well done, thou good and faithful stewards. . . ."

Many Christian families like the Durants have successfully developed and implemented strategic business continuation and succession plans. Doing so has enabled them to both effectively prepare their heirs or other successors to take over the business while also passing it to them free of any capital gains, gift or estate tax liabilities. There are many solutions to this stewardship dilemma for those who are prepared to proactively plan for this inevitable transfer. The sooner you begin working on this dilemma, the easier it will be to solve.

Navigating Dilemma #6

How Can I Best Render unto Caesar *and* unto God?

—៣—

As Benjamin Franklin's old saying goes, "in this world nothing is certain but *death and taxes*." This mindset has obviously been around for a very long time—long before our current tax laws came into existence. Our government taxes you when you make it (income tax), when you buy it (sales tax), when you sell it (capital gains tax), and then when you die (estate tax).

The government is our ever-present co-worker, business partner, and heir. It is the largest non-profit organization in America. The good news is, though, Ben was wrong. As a Christian, God has a solution for the *death* problem and there are also creative solutions for the *tax* problem.

About forty years ago U. S. Appeals Court Justice, Learned Hand, made this now well known statement, "In America there are two tax systems, one for the informed and one for the uninformed. Both systems are legal."

Uninformed taxpayers reluctantly turn over vastly greater portions of their wealth to the federal government than they need to. Judge Hand goes on to say,

> Anyone may arrange his affairs so that his taxes shall be as low as possible; he is not bound to choose that pattern which best pays the treasury. There is not even a patriotic duty to increase one's taxes. Over and over again the courts have said that there is nothing sinister in arranging affairs as to keep taxes as low as possible. Everyone does it, rich and poor alike, and all do right, for nobody owes any public duty to pay more than the law demands.[7]

What very few people understand is that some taxes are optional and are only paid by the uninformed or the unmotivated—in other words, only those who do not know or do not care pay these taxes.

For example, were you aware that capital gains taxes are optional? Have you ever paid capital gains taxes on the sale of an asset? Why? Was it because you wanted to pay the tax? Or, was it because you didn't want to take the time to structure the transaction to avoid it? Or, was it because you didn't even know avoiding it was an option?

Keep in mind, what makes the capital gains tax so onerous is not only the tax itself, but the loss of the use of those tax monies for the rest of your life. Let me give

---

[7] For more on "Are You an Informed or an Uniformed Taxpayer?" see my books, *Spiritual Thoughts on Material Things* and *Family Wealth Counseling: Getting to the Heart of the Matter*.

you a real life example. Let's say you are fifty-five years old and you sell a $2 million asset with no basis. Your capital gains tax on that sale would be $300,000. With a life expectancy of twenty-five more years and a growth rate of seven percent, that $300,000 would grow to $1.6 million before you relocate (to heaven). So, $1.6 million is the real economic cost of selling that asset and incurring the needless capital gains tax.

If that capital gains tax had not been paid, the family would have retained that $1.6 million to be used by the family or given to support Kingdom causes. Multiply this by any number of sales of appreciated assets over a lifetime and the cumulative economic loss to the family—and to the Kingdom—is massive.

Now, what if I told you that if you choose to arrange the sale of this asset so as *not to pay* capital gains tax, the Federal Government would also give you an income tax deduction to boot? What if I told you that the IRS would give you an additional $200,000 income tax deduction that you could use against other income you earned in that same year? In a forty percent tax bracket you would save $80,000 that you can now keep in your pocket and not send to the IRS.

Assuming that you invest those funds in the same way you invested the capital gains tax savings that would add another $435,000 to your family's assets for a total of $2,035,000 of retained wealth between not paying the capital gains tax and the income tax deduction—and this on the sale of only one $2 million asset!

Another way to look at this scenario would be to see what it would produce in the way of additional annual income.

A tax savings of $380,000 invested at seven percent would give you just over $26,000 every year for the rest of your life—adding to your expected total lifetime income an additional $650,000.

My question is this, "Why would Christians who want to be good stewards of the wealth the Lord has entrusted to them needlessly surrender this much to our government if they do not have to?" I am convinced it is not that they do not care, but that they do not even know they have the option.

Let me also comment on another optional tax—estate taxes. I am often asked by affluent Christian couples and other professional advisors, "What do you think is going to happen with estate taxes? Are they going to go away or not?" My standard answer is, "Since they are already an optional tax, why don't you just go ahead and opt out of paying them. So, it really doesn't matter what Congress ends up doing with estate tax laws, it will have no effect on those who have planned wisely." In other words, it is better to be proactive in planning to eliminate all estate taxes instead of passively standing by, waiting on the ever-changing political maneuverings of Congress to see what, if any, estate taxes might have to be paid when you depart this life.

If you think the capital gains tax savings was impressive in the previous example, estate tax savings is more impressive still. A family worth $55 million saved over $29 million in needless estate taxes. Another family worth $25 million saved over $11 million in needless estate taxes. Yet another family worth $900 million eliminated over $390 million in needless estate taxes.

These are enormous amounts of accumulated wealth that their heirs will now continue to control and use for themselves and to support Kingdom causes. Would it not be better if they supported something God cares about instead of voluntarily sending these monies to the IRS never to be seen or heard from again?

Even more troubling for those of us who are Christians is that much of what will be done with our "contributions" to the Federal Government are things to which we will be ethically, morally, and spiritually opposed. But one thing you can be sure of, they will not be calling us to ask what they should do with our contributions!

I think it is safe to say that of all the things we do with our annual income, our payments to the IRS are the least enjoyable "expenditure." Yet, we have found over the past three decades that one hundred percent of all the families we have encountered have been unknowingly donating substantially more to the IRS annually than was necessary.[8]

If you are paying more in income taxes than you want, if you are going to pay any capital gains taxes ever, or if your present wealth distribution plan still has you paying any amount of gift or estate taxes, then I can say with absolute certainty you have more tax planning to do if you want to maximize the wise stewardship of all that the Lord has entrusted to you.

Substantial annual income tax savings often comes as a surprise to many families. It is usually a very significant

---

[8] From "Don't Render Unto Caesar More than You Owe," in my book, *Spiritual Thoughts on Material Things.*

planning "bonus" that they had not fully expected when they began the planning process.

It is only good stewardship to do all we can to legally reduce the income taxes we must pay to the IRS. And let me add that the difference between income tax avoidance and income tax evasion is about fifteen years in Leavenworth! We are talking about tax avoidance here. Employing common, often-used, time-tested, creative-planning techniques will substantially reduce income taxes—all as a direct result of having developed a comprehensive and integrated Master Stewardship Plan.

"The proof is in the pudding," as the old saying goes. So, here are some real life examples of what some families have saved in income taxes. (The names have obviously been changed to protect the wealthy!)

Walter and Sue are independently wealthy and devote their full-time efforts to ministering to pastors in very creative ways. As a result of developing a comprehensive, strategic Master Stewardship Plan, they are now saving an additional $300,000 per year in annual income taxes. This $300,000 now remains in their pockets and under their control instead of going into the coffers of the Federal Government. Consequently, their capacity to minister to pastors has increased by over $300,000 a year!

Tom and Betty were owners of a growing business and needed to develop a strategic Master Stewardship Plan that would enable them to (1) pass on their family business to the next generation who were already involved, (2) maintain their current lifestyle, and (3) enable them to support Kingdom causes that they cared about in a significant way.

The implementation of their strategic Master Stewardship Plan produced over $230,000 in increased income tax savings for them in the first five years and $700,000 over the rest of their lives.

Rick and Mark together with their wives jointly own a very successful family business. They needed a business continuation plan to get the business to the next generation. They were also facing devastating estate taxes that would severely cripple, if not kill, the business. Both couples were committed Christians who had an earnest desire to support Kingdom causes. They developed an inter-generational Master Stewardship Plan that achieved those objectives. The fringe benefit to the plan was that it saved them over $1.4 million in income taxes over the first five years and almost $11 million over the rest of their lives.

Another significant note in all these stories is that these families are now going to be giving a combined $200 million away to support the cause of Christ during the rest of their lives and also after they relocate.

In addition to the income tax savings and the increased Kingdom giving from implementing their respective plans, each of these couples' net, spendable incomes actually increased, and their children would now be receiving the exact inheritance they wanted them to have.

All of these positive outcomes were achieved because these families took the time and made the effort to develop a well thought-out, integrated Master Stewardship Plan for themselves and their heirs. Do not think that just because you have a competent accountant you are taking full advantage of all the income tax planning options available to you. That could be a very costly—and erroneous—assumption.

Remember, strategic planning is far more than just avoiding taxes. The ultimate objective is to deploy God's material blessings to causes that are on God's heart.

Navigating the
Giving Dilemmas
Affluent Christians Face

—ɷ—

Navigating Dilemma #7

How Much Should I Be Giving and When?

—ⷶⷶ—

The affluent Christian families we have met and worked with over the years all recognize that their business and financial success was not due solely to their personal genius and extraordinary hard work. Yes, their abundant financial success has been partially due to these factors, but it has also been due to direct blessings from the hand of God as well. They openly acknowledge that they have accumulated far more wealth and prosperity than their personal efforts should have ever produced for them. They also understand that there are many people in this world who have worked just as hard and just as long as they have, yet these people have not succeeded in accumulating any significant amounts of wealth whatsoever.

We often hear these holders of wealth use the word "blessed" to describe the reason for their substantial, accumulation of possessions. Even when I used to work with unbelievers years ago, they would use words like "fortunate" or "lucky" to describe their financial success, acknowledging that their achievements were not all due to themselves.

When Moses is talking to the children of Israel prior to their entry into the Promised Land, Moses warns them of the danger of erroneously thinking, *"My power and the strength of my hand made me this wealth"* (Deuteronomy 8:17). He goes on to remind them in no uncertain terms that it is God *"who is giving you power to make wealth"* (v. 18). Solomon reconfirms this same idea in Proverbs 10:22, *"It is the blessing of the LORD that makes rich."*

No one, rich or poor, would question the blessings that accompany the possession of great wealth, but there is another side to that blessing, and Jesus identifies it very clearly for us in Luke 12:48 NIV, *"From everyone who has been given much, much will be demanded; and from the one who has been entrusted with much, much more will be asked."* The *blessing* of great wealth also carries with it a great *responsibility*.

However, there is a hindrance to fully embracing that responsibility for many wealthy Christians, and it is taught in most churches. It is something that sets a limit on their giving rather than turning them loose to accomplish all that is in their hearts to do for the Kingdom. That teaching is known as *the tithe.*[9]

The idea of tithing (giving ten percent of our increase) as the standard for acceptable giving has so permeated the church that no one (including pastors and elders) questions its validity or application to those of us who are living on

---

[9] Much of the following section is from "Tithing: The Enemy of Generosity" in my book, *Spiritual Thoughts on Material Things.*

this side of the cross. Many pastors and preachers emphasize tithing in hopes that their congregations will increase their giving above the national average of Evangelicals, which is three percent. They believe that if they could just get everyone in their congregation to start tithing, the church would have more money than it needed in order to do all that it wanted to do.

Consequently, pastors fervently teach tithing as the *floor* at which every Christian ought to *start* their giving—the minimum entry point. I know of one church in my town that requires attendees to commit to tithing in order to become members. Pastors are not really aware that while their efforts to promote tithing might increase giving for a few, it actually ends up doing more harm than good to everyone in their congregation.

Let me illustrate. Take any congregation that is being consistently and regularly indoctrinated with tithing as the giving standard. Those who, for whatever reason—good or bad—are not able or willing to tithe are made to feel guilty that they are giving less than they "owe" God. So their giving is accompanied with feelings of guilt because they are told they are "robbing God." (See Malachi 3:8.)

Then you have those who are tithing to the penny. If they get a paycheck for $3,125.60, they will write a check to the church for $312.56. They are content to give exactly what they have been taught God has prescribed for them to give. Their giving will only increase as their income increases (mathematically to the penny).

Then there are those rare few who have broken over the tithe standard taught by the church and are now giving over ten percent. They often look upon themselves with some sense of pride because they are actually exceeding the required, minimum standard of giving.

Now let me ask you, which of these attitudes of giving is healthy—giving with guilt, giving legalistically to the penny, or giving with pride?

You see, as soon as you employ some mathematical formula to determine how much someone ought to be giving—to determine what God expects—you actually create spiritual, psychological, and emotional barriers to *generous giving*. We are all fallen, sinful creatures and consequently want to know what the "rules" are because we want to please God. How much church attendance, prayer time, scripture reading, giving, etc. will be enough to keep God happy with us? So, if we accept a formula for giving, we will use it as the predetermined acceptable standard and no longer feel any need to *seek out God's will for our personal giving*.

However, the New Testament never mentions tithing as the rule and standard for New Testament Christian giving—not even one verse. There is a very good reason for this. The New Testament calls Christians to give *by faith* (life) and not give *by law* (death). (See Romans 8:2.) How much I decide to give of what the Lord has entrusted to me is just as intimately personal and individual as every other aspect of my Christian life.

To put this into perspective, let me ask:
- Has God prescribed how many minutes I must pray each day?
- Has He stipulated how many verses He expects me to read each week?

- Has He established how many people I am required to witness to each month?

The answer is an obvious "No" to all of them. God has prescribed none of these as His "acceptable standard" for being a "good Christian." Rather it is left up to each of us individually to seek out the Lord *by faith* and allow Him to direct us in how much of these activities we should be participating in.

Similarly, our giving is to be arrived at by careful, personal self-examination and seeking the Lord's direction in how much we should give as we evaluate this crucial area of financial stewardship. May I suggest that 2 Corinthians 9:7 gives us the Christian methodology for deciding how much we personally should be giving back to the Lord, not the scriptures of the Old Testament on tithing. Paul instructs, *"Each man should give what he has decided in his heart to give"* (NIV). In other words, the amount of our giving proceeds *from our heart*, not from our calculator. Our giving is to grow out of a personal relationship with Christ and not merely a prescriptive formula arrived at mathematically.

I would be remiss not to mention the "rest of the story" of 2 Corinthians 9:7 as well. Paul concludes this verse by giving us the emotional outcome of giving generously by faith vs. giving legalistically by math. He says, *"Each man should give what he has decided in his heart to give, not reluctantly or under compulsion, for God loves a cheerful giver"* (NIV). Giving legalistically according to a formula too often produces a reluctant giver who is giving out of compulsion. Giving generously by faith produces a cheerful giver who is giving out of overflowing joy. Paul says this giver is the one whom God loves. I personally opt for the latter. How about you?[10]

Being Truly Blessed

It should be obvious that the primary reason the Lord has entrusted certain people with great wealth is not to simply allow them to enjoy a luxurious and opulent lifestyle. In fact, may I suggest that the fundamental motivation and primary purpose for accumulating wealth should be to *give it away*. Wealthy people will discover the greatest joy and blessing this life has to offer by using what they have accumulated to make a difference in other people's lives.

This rather revolutionary notion is clearly laid upon a strong, biblical foundation. Paul tells Timothy in 1 Timothy 6:17-19,

Instruct those who are rich in this present world not to be conceited or to fix their hope on the uncertainty of riches, but on God, who richly supplies us with all things to enjoy. Instruct them to do good, to be rich in good works, to be generous and ready to share, storing up for themselves the treasure of a good foundation for the future, so that they may take hold of that which is life indeed.

---

[10] From "Tithing: The Enemy of Generosity" in my book, *Spiritual Thoughts on Material Things*.

Notice *life indeed* is realized not in the personal enjoyment of the wealth that has been accumulated, but in how much of this wealth is being shared with others. This leads to another real dilemma that wealthy Christians must address as part of their responsibilities, which is, "How much should I give away and when?"

To adequately address this dilemma, we must return to our question of chapter one, "How much of my accumulated wealth is actually surplus wealth?"—wealth that can be given away now or be invested so that *more* can be given away later. In order to answer this question, we must also return to the two questions:

1) "How much is enough for us to maintain our present lifestyle?" and
2) "How much is enough to leave our loved ones as an inheritance?"

Until you can answer these two questions, you will never be able to answer the question of how much you can spare for Kingdom work.

When wealthy people have not identified how much of what they have is surplus wealth, they will always choose to give *far less than they could or even should* to bless and help others.

However, once the amount of surplus wealth is determined, then you are ready to ask this truly challenging—and *fun*—question, "Would it be better for me to give it all away now *or keep managing and growing this surplus wealth so I can give even more away later?*"

Because we are dealing with people to whom God has given the "Midas touch," this is really a legitimate question. They can indeed grow wealth very effectively and often quite rapidly. This "gift" dramatically complicates the question of how much to give and when.

To illustrate the potential impact of the time value of money, consider if you could grow money at a rate of say, twenty-four percent (which many wealth-builders can achieve in their specific area of business expertise) for ten years. Doing that would grow $100,000 to a whopping $860,000. Now, would it be better to give the $100,000 now or to wait ten years and give $860,000 away? To make the decision even more challenging, in twenty years that $100,000 could grow to almost $7.4 million. So, is it better to give $100,000 now or $7.4 million in twenty years?

Now, do not misunderstand what we are addressing here. We are not debating whether this wealth will be given, but *when* it will be given. Based upon the wealth-builder's ability to grow his accumulated surplus wealth, when and how they can best bless the Kingdom of God is not as simple as it might appear on the surface. They can properly ask, "Should we give less now, or grow it and give a whole lot more away later?" Answering this involves plugging into God's plan as well as some real creative thinking. It is a challenging process, but ultimately very rewarding.

This dilemma becomes even more challenging when you consider that people and ministries have needs today that require immediate support. And if that support, even if it would be a much greater amount, does not come until many years later, the ministry or opportunity may no longer exist.

This question of *when* to give must be addressed with careful thought and prayer. Families can gain clarity on this issue by developing a Giving Master Plan that answers these kinds of difficult giving questions:

- Who do we give to?
- When do we give to them?
- What do we want them to do with it?
- How much will we give them?

In addition to these, there are a host of other related issues that a family must consider to maximize the impact of their giving and help them enjoy "life indeed."

Navigating Dilemma #8

Sacrificial Giving

—∭—

One of the most difficult challenges affluent Christians must face is how to experience the joy and blessing of *sacrificial* giving when they possess so much surplus wealth. We must not forget when Jesus sat down by the temple treasury and observed people putting in their offerings—the rich depositing their "large sums" and the poor widow dropping in "*two small copper coins*." Jesus offers a rather shocking assessment of what He saw. He said,

> *"Truly I say to you, this poor widow put in more than all of them; for they all out of their surplus put into the offering; but she out of her poverty put in all that she had to live on."*
>
> *Luke 21:1-4*

By this statement Jesus is setting up a new method for evaluating generosity. Here He is saying, "Your generosity is not based upon how much you give, it is based upon *how much you have left over after you give.*" The giving of these rich men had absolutely no impact on their lifestyles whatsoever. It was entirely surplus wealth. But the widow's giving affected her lifestyle that very day.

The ancient concept of tithing is not really equal in that giving ten percent of $1 million is not the same as giving ten percent of $10,000. According to the Old Testament law of tithing, ten percent is ten percent regardless of the amount being tithed from. But with Jesus' new insights here, we now understand that sacrificial giving has more to do with the ninety percent than it does the ten percent. In other words, it would be far easier for a person to tithe $100,000 of their million-dollar income because they would still have $900,000 left over to "eek" out a living. While after tithing on $10,000, that person would only have $9,000 left to live on. This is the point Jesus is trying to make here: "Look at what you have left over to judge your generosity, not what you are giving."

I can tell you with certainty that a poor woman who chooses to sacrificially give $500 out of her meager $12,000 annual Social Security income is being substantially more generous than the businessman who is giving $50,000 of his $350,000 annual income, even though the woman is giving only four percent and the businessman is giving fourteen percent.[11]

Occasionally, I have been asked by affluent people, "How much should we be giving?" They sense that ten percent is

---

[11] Much of the following section is from "Tithing: The Enemy of Generosity" in my book, *Spiritual Thoughts on Material Things*.

no longer the right percentage for them and they are looking for someone to give them what that right percentage should be. My answer is always the same, "That is a very important question. Unfortunately, you are asking it of the wrong person. You need to ask that question to the One who owns all your stuff."

Many pastors I have talked with about generosity vs. tithing express the same gnawing concern. They fear that if they tell their congregation they are not required to tithe, the church's weekly offerings will collapse. I disagree. If believers were properly taught and really came to understand and live out the idea of *generous giving by faith* instead of *legalistic giving by math*, I believe that Christians' giving would explode. It may not happen overnight, because the church will have to overcome years of bad teaching, but once people really understand they need to go to their knees to decide how much to give instead of their calculators, we will likely see another outbreak of generosity that might compare to what the Israelites experienced in the construction of the Tabernacle. Their giving was so "over the top" Moses had to command them to stop giving. (See Exodus 35:20-36:7.)

I recently attended a meeting in which the speaker was enthusiastically telling about a financial advisor who had a wealthy client selling a $1.5 million asset, and the advisor had asked him about tithing on the sale price to the Kingdom, which he ended up doing. What struck me as unfortunate in this story is that the advisor did not ask his client if he personally needed any of the sale proceeds. Maybe he should have given one hundred percent of the sale proceeds to the Kingdom—and if not one hundred percent, how much might

God want to use of these funds for His purposes? Possibly an even more challenging question for this client to ask himself would be, "How much of this $1.5 million would I have to give away for the gift to be a real, sacrificial act of faith on my part?"

The first option—the tithe—is clean, mathematically simple and requires little thought. The second—generosity—is neither clean nor simple and requires genuine soul searching, faith testing and "wrestling with God." In our struggle to find an amount right for giving each week, we might find ourselves feeling compelled to ask a similar question, "How much would I have to give to the Lord in order for my giving to be both generous and sacrificial?"

That may be why the Old Testament concept of tithing was replaced with a different criterion for giving in the New Testament. First, if we insist on following the letter of the Old Testament law, we need to understand that there were actually three tithes required. Two tithes were annual and another was every third year. So, the Old Testament tithing law actually required giving an average of 23.33 percent of annual increase. Second, these tithes were collected partially to underwrite Israel's theocratic governmental services. So, Old Testament tithing was a form of national taxation—they also had their own IRS (Israeli Revenue Service). Third, the Old Testament tithing amount was to be based upon the family's cumulative possessions (net worth), not just their annual earned income.

Then, of course, a good legalist will also need to answer a number of interesting questions such as,

- Do we tithe off our net or our gross? and

- When we sell an appreciated asset, since the money we used to invest in it was "after tithe" money, do we now need to tithe off the entire sale price or just the capital gain?

These kinds of questions are reserved for members of "Legalists Anonymous," but are totally irrelevant to the New Testament concept of giving.

The Old Testament concept is giving *by law*. The New Testament concept is giving *by faith*. The opposite of giving *by faith* is giving *by sight*. So, if you know you can afford to give a certain amount to the Lord, are you giving *by sight* or *by faith*? You can see the challenge here. For many wealthy Christians, it has been a very long time since they have given to the Lord by faith.

C. S. Lewis, the great Christian apologist and author of the well-known *Chronicles of Narnia* series, said in his book *Mere Christianity*,

> I do not believe one can settle how much we ought to give. I am afraid the only safe rule is to give more than we can spare. In other words, if our expenditures on comforts, luxuries, amusements, etc. is up to the standard common among those with the same income as our own, we are probably giving away too little. If our charities do not at all pinch or hamper us, I should say they are too small.

The probing question confronting all of us with surplus wealth is, "If we stop giving by the law and start giving by faith, how do we decide how much we should give?" Let me ask you another question that might help clarify this. If I were to ask you to give one dollar a week to the Lord, would you be comfortable committing to do so? Obviously you would, because giving one dollar a week requires no faith on your part. You can give it entirely by sight. But what if I asked you to start giving $1 million a week to the Lord? You might swallow hard and admit that you really do not believe you can do that. You see, we have just moved beyond faith. We do not think we can give that much even with God's help. And trying to give beyond faith is just as futile as giving with no faith at all. So, the goal is for our giving to be at a level that requires us to trust God to take care of us while we concentrate on taking care of others.

And once we see that we have achieved giving at this new *by faith* level, something immediately changes. That new level of giving is now no longer *by faith*, because that level of giving has now become giving *by sight*. So now, how much do you need to increase your giving to be able to continue to give *by faith*? It is at this point that you will encounter the true blessing of giving—when it has stretched you to give more than just your unneeded surplus wealth.

The diagram below illustrates this concept of giving by faith and how God will not fully bless our giving without faith (because the amount is too little or too great). So, our prayer should be the same as the Apostles, "*Increase our faith*" (Luke 17:5).

New Testament Concept of Giving by Faith

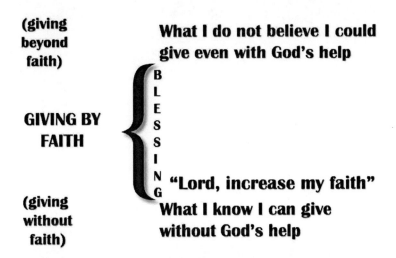

(giving beyond faith)

What I do not believe I could give even with God's help

GIVING BY FAITH

BLESSING

(giving without faith)

"Lord, increase my faith"
What I know I can give without God's help

I learned this lesson about "by faith" giving many years ago from a ten-year-old boy named Jimmy Mitchell. One Sunday before church, I was standing up at the pulpit getting my sermon notes ready and Jimmy came running into the auditorium. He ran up to me with a dollar bill in his hand and said, "Jay, look what I've got." I said, "Jimmy, that's great. Where did you get it?" He told me that after he mowed his yard, he decided to go ahead and mow old Mrs. Brown's yard next door. "After I finished, she came out and gave me this dollar." He went on to say, "Jay, I'd like to give some of it to the Lord."

I replied, "Jimmy, I know the Lord would be so pleased that you would want to share some of that dollar with Him. How much do you think you would like to give?"

Even after roughly three decades, I still remember what he said to me like it was yesterday. He looked down at the dollar and then questioningly looked up at me and said, "Do you think He would mind if I kept a dime?"

His words still ring in my mind, "*Do you think He would mind if I kept a dime?*" Imagine what would happen to the kingdom of God if we were all to begin thinking and acting like Jimmy Mitchell.

Let me offer some challenging suggestions on how you might begin in at least some meaningful way to experience giving *by faith*.

- ✓ Make your Kingdom giving proportional to what you personally consume on your lifestyle (i.e. for every dollar you spend on your personal lifestyle, you will give one dollar for Kingdom work).
- ✓ Reduce your current lifestyle consumption to increase current annual funding of Kingdom causes.
- ✓ Sell assets that you currently use for your lifestyle and give the proceeds to support Kingdom causes.
- ✓ Forego a planned purchase or expense and give what would have been the cost to fund the Kingdom.
- ✓ Purchase a less expensive product than you normally would and give the difference to support a Kingdom organization.
- ✓ Give all growth of your net worth over a specific amount to Kingdom outreaches annually.

✓ And if you really want to get radical, consider what Jesus said to the rich, young ruler, *"Sell all that you possess and distribute it to the poor, and you shall have treasure in heaven; and come, follow Me"* (Luke 18:22).

Remember what Jesus said, *"From everyone who has been given much, much will be required; and to whom they entrusted much, of him they will ask all the more"* (Luke 12:48). Are we giving *by faith* all that we should be giving from all that we have been given?

Navigating Dilemma #9

Having a Master Giving Strategy

—᙭ᙡ—

One of the most exciting aspects of developing and implementing a Master Stewardship Plan is answering the question, "What should we do with all that we have to give away?"

After all, this is the pivotal question of stewardship, "How do we use what we have to build the Kingdom of God?" The stewardship of wealth was a central teaching of Christ. In fact, Jesus spoke more in scripture about handling money and material things than He did about sin and salvation. The reason seems obvious to me. He knows where we all live each day of our lives. Stuff is a central part of life. As believers we need to know what the Bible says about financial matters such as:

- taxes (see Luke 20:25, Romans 13:7),
- inheritances (see Proverbs 17:16, 19:10a),
- debt (see Proverbs 22:7),
- generous giving (see Luke 6:38),
- accumulating possessions (see Proverbs 18:11),

- investment diversification (see Ecclesiastes 11:1-2),
- hoarding wealth (see Ecclesiastes 5:13),
- financial integrity (see Proverbs 11:1, 10:2a), and
- the consequences of planning your life around your stuff (see Matthew 16:26).

It is not enough, however, to just know what the Bible says about such topics, you must also integrate all of these biblical directives into a comprehensive Master Stewardship Plan.[12]

You will also want to make sure your plans are based on sound biblical wisdom as we have already touched upon in previous chapters. This means also considering the following truths:

- God owns everything and it is our sole job as trustees to find out what God wants us to do with all the stuff He has entrusted to us (see Psalm 24:1);
- It is more blessed to give than to receive (see Acts 20:35);
- "Life indeed" comes from being generous and not from holding on to our wealth for our own consumption and pleasure (see 1 Timothy 6:17-19);

---

[12] For more on biblical standards by which to evaluate your advisors, see "Are Your Advisors Asking You the Right Questions?" and other chapters in my book, *Spiritual Thoughts on Material Things*. Also see chapter 19, "Assembling an Effective Planning Team" in my book *Family Wealth Counseling: Getting to the Heart of the Matter*.

- A person's ability to make wealth comes from God and is not the result of one's personal genius and hard work (see Deuteronomy 8:17-18);
- Poorly thought out and excessive inheritances can destroy the very people we love the most (see Proverbs 20:21 and Ecclesiastes 2:18-19, 21);
- The best financial investment a person can make is in the Kingdom and the "profits" from those investments will be stored up and waiting for us when we relocate to our permanent home to enjoy for eternity (see Matthew 6:19-21); and
- Accumulating wealth solely for our own ease and comfort leaves us—as defined by God—a "fool" (see Luke 12:16-21).

Many Christian families have been regular givers over their lifetimes, but their new awareness of their substantially greater capacity to give leaves them facing a whole new series of difficult giving dilemmas. As a wealthy man once said to me, "It is one thing to give away $50,000, but it is an entirely different thing to give $1 million away each year. That is going to be a real challenge!"

The idea that a family now has many millions of dollars to invest in Kingdom work starting now and continuing even beyond their eternal relocation is something they never imagined possible. So, needless to say, they have spent little time and even less effort addressing these issues in any serious way.

As the awareness of this new reality of giving sets into their thinking, a myriad of questions begin pouring into their minds:

1) Do we want to set up a family foundation? And if so, which of the seven different kinds of family foundations is best for our family?

2) What ministries can we partner with to help us impact the world in our areas of interest?

3) What should our foundation's mission statement be?

4) Do we want to give it all away now or do we want to build an endowment and give all the income away until Jesus' return?

5) Do we want to make a few really large gifts or do we want to make a large number of smaller gifts?

6) Who in our family do we want to include in working with us on the foundation?

7) Should we set up an advisory team to help in operating our foundation?

8) How do we make strategic decisions as to the amount and frequency of our giving?

9) How personally involved can our family become in giving of our time and talents as well as our treasures to support Kingdom work?

10) Would it be good to set up a junior board of our foundation so our grandchildren can start learning and growing?

11) Can we actually do ministry ourselves and be supported by our own foundation?

12) Should our foundation exist into perpetuity or should there be a point in time at which it terminates? (After all, I have heard so many horror stories of family foundations that have been hijacked by liberals and the foundation now supports causes the founders would be totally opposed to.)

It is at this time that the founders of the family fortune begin to realize the heavy burden that falls on them as they are reminded of Jesus' words, "*From everyone who has been given much, much will be required*" (Luke 12:48). How do you even begin to think about giving millions of dollars away wisely and effectively? Most start out on this journey as complete novices in this area of mega-stewardship.

I remember the story an attorney shared with me many years ago. One of his clients was a widowed man who had amassed a substantial fortune over his lifetime. He and his deceased wife had no children, only a niece and a nephew who were both very troubled kids. He decided that he did not want them to get any of his wealth and he did not want to pay any estate taxes, so he concluded that he would give his entire estate away to charity when he died. The attorney asked him who he wanted to receive his wealth. The elderly man said, "That's a very hard question and I don't think I am ready to answer that yet, but I will be giving it serious thought and get back with you."

A few months passed and the attorney called to see if he had yet made his charitable beneficiary choices. The man again hesitated, "No, I have been giving it a lot of thought, but I just can't decide where to give it."

It was about three months later when the attorney sat down at the breakfast table, opened the newspaper and read the headlines that one of the community's most prominent citizens, this very client, had passed away the night before. Now the multimillions of wealth that he had every intention of giving away to help ministries and non-profits would end up going to the two places he most did not want any of it to go—to the IRS and to his niece and nephew—all because he could not finally decide where, how or to whom to give it.

Aristotle may have said it best. He observed,

> To give away money is an easy matter and in any man's power. But to decide to whom to give it and how large and when, and for what purpose and how, is neither in every man's power—nor an easy matter. Hence it is that such excellence is rare, praiseworthy, and noble.

It is this same ancient dilemma that still troubles affluent families today. Having a Giving Master Plan will help affluent families not just acknowledge that they now have huge sums of wealth to give away, but to actually "pull the trigger" and do it—and to do it well.

The words that I think all of us most want to hear as we stand before our gracious, Heavenly Father as He evaluates how well we managed what He had entrusted to us are "Well done." Our ultimate goal should be to someday hear from God, "Well done! You have been faithful with what I entrusted to you." That will be a sweet day!

Navigating Dilemma #10

Surrendering All to Christ

—◆—

One of the most famous hymns of all time is "I Surrender All." The words are, "All to Jesus I surrender, all to Him I freely give." Easy to sing, very difficult to live. I think for most Christians, regardless of their economic station in life, we might more honestly sing, "*Some* to Jesus I surrender, *some* to Him I freely give..." This challenging idea of total surrender of all we are and all we have takes on new dimensions for those whom the Lord has blessed with substantial material possessions.

Affluent followers of Jesus often limit their involvement in Kingdom work to little more than financial support. And because wealthy Christians normally have far more money than anything else, when they consider how to best support Kingdom causes, they naturally look to their surplus wealth as an easy way to make the greatest difference. This mindset may be natural, but it is anything but supernatural.

I have always been struck by Paul's comments about the Macedonian Church in 2 Corinthians 8:1-5. At that time the entire region of Macedonia was struggling through a

multi-year famine that had wreaked devastating consequences for everyone, including the local church. Paul
reports to us,

> *And now, brothers, we want you to know about the*
> *grace that God has given the Macedonian churches.*
> *Out of the most severe trial, their overflowing joy*
> *and their extreme poverty welled up in rich gener-*
> *osity. For I testify that they gave as much as they*
> *were able, and even beyond their ability. Entirely on*
> *their own, they urgently pleaded with us for the privi-*
> *lege of sharing in this service to the saints. And they*
> *did not do as we expected, but they gave themselves*
> *first to the Lord* (NIV).

Talk about "I surrender all!" Here we have believers who
are struggling to just stay alive through extreme, desperate
circumstances. Yet in the midst of that, their passion to
advance the work of God so overwhelmed them that they
ended up giving far more—from a worldly perspective—
than they should have given. That, of course, is both impressive and inspiring for all of us. What really strikes me is not
the amount of their giving, but what motivated them to that
level of giving. In other words, how was it that they were
so energized to give excessively of their meager material
possessions? Paul tells us and this is the point I am trying to
make here, *"they did not* [give] *as we expected, but they gave*
themselves first to the Lord."

The greatest gift we have to give to the Lord of all our
earthly possessions is *ourselves*. And for those with abun-

dance, it is far too easy to think that donating a meaningful sum of financial treasure somehow permits us to opt out of most, if not all, personal involvement in ministry. We can easily afford the money, but the time and talents that God has blessed and entrusted to us seem far more costly.

This kind of erroneous thinking is similar to what happened with army conscripts during the Civil War. A person of means, if drafted, would simply hire someone else to take his place. In other words, he would simply buy his way out of the war. May I suggest that Jesus is far more interested in our personal involvement in ministry (the war) than He is in our financial support of it, no matter how significant that financial support might be?

I am not at all suggesting that personal involvement in ministry should be disconnected from our God-given passions, talents, and life-experiences. To the contrary, these should be the very things from which our personal ministry flows. And God knows that whatever passions, talents, and life-experience He has given to us, there are a myriad of ministries that desperately need what we could personally bring to the table.

Ministries are in serious need of men and women who are visionaries, "out of the box" thinkers, movers and shakers, who can provide business expertise and financial savvy. These are abilities and experiences that ministries simply cannot buy.

It also seems that all too often affluent people who have substantial surplus wealth typically struggle to know how and where to give it (often because there is so much to give away). And this dilemma is present because they are not spiritually, emotionally, and physically connected in any significant way in giving of themselves to any particular Kingdom work.

What Is Your Most Valuable Possession?[13]

Many years ago I heard Bob Buford, a self-made multi-millionaire and author of the book *Halftime: Changing your Game Plan from Success to Significance*, speak at a conference. Right in the middle of the presentation he made a comment that was so profound and struck me so deeply that I do not think I really heard anything else he said for the rest of his presentation. He paused, gave a reflective look, and then commented, "It seems insane to me that a person would be willing to trade what he has a shortage of—time—in order to gain more of what he already has a surplus of—wealth." You cannot read this once and fully absorb it, so look at it again. "It seems insane to me that a person would be willing to trade what he has a shortage of—time—in order to gain more of what he already has a surplus of—wealth."

So, what is your most valuable asset? It is the time that you still have "banked" in this life. Your "time on this earth" account is all too quickly shrinking with every day that passes. And the most troubling part of this time account is that we cannot see how much we have left. Is it days, months, years, decades? We often hear people ask the question, "How do you spend your time…?" This is a very accurate way to phrase how we use our time: we *spend* it. Unlike

---

[13] Much of the following section is from "What is Your Most Valuable Possession?" in my book, *Spiritual Thoughts on Material Things*.

your financial accounts that you can make additional deposits into and build the account in the future, you can make no additional deposits into your time account. The total number of days allotted to us was deposited into our time account before we were even conceived. King David confirms this in Psalm 139:16, when he acknowledges, "*And in Your book were written all the days that were ordained for me, when as yet there was not one of them.*" So, all of us will spend our time on something—and once it is spent, it is gone.

It seems to me that we need to manage our time account with even greater care than we manage our investment accounts. We should be very leery about making any withdrawals out of our limited time account—"spending our time" in order to make additional deposits into our already substantial investment accounts.

When I was a young boy, I spent a good bit of time visiting my grandmother. She was a zealous and committed Christian woman and everywhere you turned in her small home, there were signs of her faith—a Bible on the coffee table—plaques and pictures on the walls—Bible verses on the refrigerator. There was one plaque in particular that made a significant impact on my thinking as a young boy. I did not realize it then, but I do now. The little plaque read, "Only one life 'twill soon be past, only what's done for Christ will last." My entire life, for the most part, has been one continuous effort to use the brief time that God has allotted me to do something that will have an eternal impact. Without this ultimate, eternal objective, life is correctly summed up by Solomon, "*All of it is meaningless, a chasing after the wind*" (Ecclesiastes 2:17 NIV).

What is your most valuable asset? How are you using your most valuable asset to do something that will last for eternity? Our cry should be, to paraphrase Isaiah 6:8, "Here I am Lord, [*spend*] me"

In Matthew 6:21 Jesus said, "*Where your treasure is, there your heart will be also.*" The opposite is also true, "Where your heart is, there will be your treasure also." The point is your money and your heart will *always* find themselves abiding in the same places.

Knowing where to give, how to give, when to give, for what to give, and a host of other difficult concerns can best be resolved by asking one simple question, "Where does God want me to personally invest my passions, my talents, my time, and my life-experiences to impact the Kingdom." Once you answer where you want to invest your *life* in ministry, God will clearly reveal to you where He wants you to invest your *money* as well.

Other Books by E. G. "Jay" Link

—⚏—

Spiritual Thoughts on Material Things: Thirty Days of Food for Thought, Longwood, FL, Xulon Press., 2009. (Available at www.KardiaPlanning.com or Amazon.com.)

Family Wealth Counseling: Getting to the Heart of the Matter. Franklin, IN: Professional Mentoring Program, 1999. (Available at www.KardiaPlanning.com or Amazon.com.)

Kardia, Inc.
5237 SR 144
Mooresville, IN 46158
317-831-7200
www.KardiaPlanning.com

Additional Reading to Help You Navigate

—m—

Alcorn, Randy. *The Law of Rewards*. Wheaton, Ill: Tyndale House, 2003.

Alcorn, Randy. *The Treasure Principle: Unlocking the Secret of Joyful Giving*. Sisters: Multnomah, 2005.

Beckett, John D. *Loving Monday: Succeeding in Business Without Selling Your Soul*. New York: InterVarsity Press, 2006.

Blue, Ron, and Jeremy White. *Splitting Heirs: Giving Your Money and Things to Your Children Without Ruining Their Lives*. Grand Rapids: Northfield, 2008.

Buford, Bob. *Finishing Well: What People Who Really Live Do Differently!* New York: Integrity, 2005.

Buford, Bob. *Game Plan*. Grand Rapids: Zondervan, 1999.

Buford, Bob. *Halftime: Changing Your Game Plan From Success to Significance*. Grand Rapids: Zondervan, 1994.

Grudem, Wayne. *Business for the Glory of God: The Bible's Teaching on the Moral Goodness of Business.* New York: Crossway Books, 2003.

Stanley, Andy. *Fields of Gold.* New York: Tyndale House, 2004.

Tam, Stanley. *God Owns My Business.* New York: Horizon Books, 1991.

Organizations Serving as "Lighthouses" As You Navigate These Dilemmas

—m—

Crown Financial Ministries
(www.Crown.org)

Eternal Perspective Ministries
(www.EPM.org)

Excellence in Giving
(www.ExcellenceinGiving.com)

The Gathering
(www.TheGathering.com)

Generous Giving
(www.GenerousGiving.org)

Halftime
(www.Halftime.org)

Kingdom Advisors
(www.KingdomAdvisors.org)

National Christian Foundation
(www.NationalChristian.com)

Pinnacle Forum
(www.PinnacleForum.com)

Waterstone
(www.LivingDefined.org)

LaVergne, TN USA
02 November 2010
203118LV00001B/2/P

9 781615 790173